Under the Skin

Badger Plays Book 5

Conquistador

and The Boy at the Hotel Rudolpho

Dick Kempson

Contents:

Under the Skin - *The Plays:*

Book 1: Louise Loxton	Night Caller, The Gift, Boys Behaving Badly, Sleeping Easy, Bath Time
Book 2: Mike Gould	Ring of Blood, Animal Magic, Eco-freaks in Trouble, The Case of the Following Boy, The Sub
Book 3: Rob Brannen	Hedge Hopping, Sorting Things Out, Michael and Rahima, Into the Dark, A Swagger and A Snarl
Book 4: Mike Gould	Ten Things I Hate, Joker in the Pack, Dial-a-date, Masked Ball, The First Girl in Space
Book 5: Dick Kempson	Conquistador, The Boy at the Hotel Rudolpho
Book 6: Mike Gould	Ice Maiden, Under the Skin

Badger Publishing Limited 15 Wedgwood Gate, Pin Green Industrial Estate, Stevenage, Hertfordshire SG1 4SU
Telephone: 01438 356907. Fax: 01438 747015.
www.badger-publishing.co.uk enquiries@badger-publishing.co.uk

Under the Skin - Book 5 ISBN 1 84424 432 6

Series Editor: Mike Gould
Editor: Paul Martin
Publisher: David Jamieson
Cover design: Adam Wilmott
Cover illustration: Fabricio De Oliveira (Beehive Illustration)

Introduction

Welcome to Badger's **Under the Skin** Book 5!

These two challenging and stimulating plays are designed for enjoyment, but also to help students develop speaking and listening, drama and theatre skills. The series title also gives a clue to their focus. They both cover a range of ideas, issues, stories and situations, but each is intended to uncover how and why individuals act in the way they do. Thus, they are plays designed with the stage and acting in mind, but can equally be enjoyed as group readers.

The plays were both written with an edge to them, but it is not the issues that drive them - rather an interest in telling a good story, with characters who engage our emotions, and raise questions in our mind. Will Lewis blend or be bold? What does Stefan really need and want? And, are these characters easily defined, or like shifting sands - never quite settled and comprehensible?

The plays are designed for small group performance or class reading, although it is recommended that, for the latter, one member of the group reads the stage directions and settings. Should you choose to perform the plays, much of the setting can be dispensed with, or presented in a stylised way, as in the end, it is the story and the words that matter - and you may interpret these as you wish.

All the plays in the series are written by people who are involved, or have been involved, in practical drama work with young people aged 11-16. They are an excellent resource to support the drama objectives in the Framework for Teaching English, and prepare students for drama study at GCSE and beyond, but more importantly, it is hoped that teachers and students will find them compelling and rewarding in their own right.

CONQUISTADOR

Characters:

LEWIS	boy, aged 14
GRANT	boy, aged 14
CHLOE	girl, aged 14
ANNA	girl, aged 14
SID 'N' NANCY	boy, aged 16

SKANKY PETE does not appear in the play but can be found in the kebab shop most Friday and Saturday nights.

The play is set one month into the school year. For these students, it is the beginning of Year 10.

Scene 1 A classroom

It is a Thursday morning. GRANT is sitting at the teacher's desk, scanning some of the teacher's files. He is alone in the room. In the distance can be heard the sounds of students moving through corridors. In the opening moments of the scene this fades and it becomes quiet. It is the start of lesson one.

After a moment, LEWIS enters and waits hesitantly just inside the room.

GRANT: You Lewis?

LEWIS: Yeah.

GRANT: Come in. Shut the door.

LEWIS does so.

GRANT: (*indicating a chair in front of the teacher's desk*) Sit.

LEWIS does so. And GRANT contemplates him for a moment.

LEWIS: You're Grant?

GRANT: I am.

LEWIS: And you're supposed to be showing me round?

GRANT: All in good time.

LEWIS: OK. It's just that I'm supposed to go back to her office. You know, when we've finished the tour.

GRANT: That's at the end of the lesson. We've plenty of time for the tour.

But Mrs Reid's instructions to me were a little more involved. "Show him round" - yes. But also: "Get to know him. Make him feel at home. Help him fit in here."

LEWIS: (*sitting back in his chair and looking round*) Right. Thanks.

GRANT: It's a tall order but she knows I can deliver. I did a similar job for her in Year 9. Successful integration. Inside a month, you couldn't pick him out in a parade. Looked like he'd been here all his life. Complete waste of space but you can't have everything.

LEWIS: Look, I don't want to put you out. Show me round then I can manage myself...

GRANT: Manage yourself!? Disaster! Your first few days - hours - at a school mark you down for life. You make some early mistakes and it's too late. You're 'the kid with this' or 'the kid who does that'. And you'll never change it. Not for years anyway.

LEWIS: (*doubtfully but prepared to listen*) ...Right?

GRANT: But this can all be managed. No problem. The secret is to 'blend'.

LEWIS: Blend?

GRANT: Pass like water through water. Be invisible, one of the crowd. Then you got something...

LEWIS: What?

GRANT: Time. I can buy you time.

LEWIS: I don't understand.

GRANT: People make quick judgements. I'm just saying, be a bit invisible. Slow things down.

LEWIS: Surely people either like you or they don't?

GRANT: Not you, things about you. Example: uniform.

LEWIS: I'm not bothered about uniform.

GRANT: Fine sentiment, and just how you should be... a month after you get here. But right here, today, we gotta do something with your uniform.

LEWIS: What? It's a uniform.

GRANT: It's too new.

LEWIS: That's because it is new. I just got here, remember?

GRANT: And a new uniform is fine... as long as you're not new yourself.

When you're new, a new uniform is a sandwich board. It says: 'I don't fit in yet; I hope everyone will like me; I'm a little bit pathetic.'

When you've been around a bit, a new uniform is just that, a new uniform. It means nothing.

LEWIS: But I am new. For the next month, at least.

GRANT: Tomorrow, I'll bring trousers and an old sweatshirt, frayed at the edges. For today, give me the sweatshirt.

Reluctantly, LEWIS takes off his sweatshirt.

LEWIS: You gonna tear it up?

GRANT: Sixth form do all the cleaning in this place.

You're ever here after four o'clock, it's like a scene from *Night of the Living Dead.* They wander round with headphones on, wafting a broom. They have no idea what they're doing. Only, they're doing it very, very slowly.

And leaving piles of dust in every corner of the school.

GRANT rubs the sweatshirt into the dust in a corner by the desk and hands it back. LEWIS looks on in astonishment.

Undo your top buttons. Tie right down there.

LEWIS follows instructions.

Scuff your shoes, roll up your sleeves so they might be frayed, shirt out at the back... a bit at the front, too.

He surveys LEWIS.

GRANT: OK. That'll do till tomorrow. I mean it, I'll have those clothes. You wear them. Give them back to me in a month.

LEWIS: Do I pass?

GRANT: Not as simple as that.

It's all about how you move down a corridor from one place to the next - critical. The eyes give people away every time.

LEWIS: (*laughing*) The whites of the eyes - the fear!

GRANT: Not fear, just uncertainty. When I show you round, pay attention. Don't think: 'I get lost, I'll ask.' Figure it out in advance. Look like you know where you're going.

LEWIS: Huh?

GRANT: Do I have to spell it out? Don't stare into every face that passes trying to figure out who's here: he's short and she's fit. No. For the first few days, no curiosity. Just be going somewhere, like you know the place, like you're not interested.

LEWIS: OK.

GRANT: And, this is just an animal thing. Don't look anyone in the eye. Look them in the eye and it's a challenge. But don't look down neither. That's submission. Just look where you're going. Got it?

LEWIS: Yeah.

GRANT: Blend. Buy some time. Fit in.

Now, the tour. Give us your timetable. Nothing you don't need to know, but pay attention.

And a few things not on the official route...

They make their way to the door.

You smoke?

Scene 2 Inside the main entrance to the school

It is Thursday afternoon. The bell has just gone for the end of school. Moments before, hundreds of students have pressed through the doors here but now it is empty, except perhaps for the occasional straggler.

LEWIS is waiting by the door, clearly looking out for someone, without wishing to appear to do so.

CHLOE appears, but instead of walking past, she stops in the entrance with LEWIS.

CHLOE: You waiting for someone?

LEWIS: Yeah.

CHLOE: You gonna wait long?

LEWIS: If I have to, yeah. Maybe.

CHLOE: Friend of yours you're waiting for?

LEWIS: Kind of.

CHLOE: What's your name?

LEWIS: Lewis.

CHLOE: He's not coming.

LEWIS: What?

CHLOE: He's not coming.

LEWIS: Who?

CHLOE: Grant.

LEWIS: Oh.

A pause. Lewis is making to go.

CHLOE: He's stood you up.

LEWIS: What!

CHLOE: He's stood me up too. He doesn't mean to. He's busy. He forgets. D'you know why he's not coming?

LEWIS: No.

CHLOE: 'Course not, you wouldn't be waiting otherwise. He's playing football. For the school team. Or, rather, he's not playing football for the school team.

LEWIS: (*with uncertainty*) Right.

CHLOE: Grant is picked every game. Has been ever since Year 8. Only he never plays. No one else will play for the school team if they are going to be substitute or they're going to be substituted. Grant likes football but he can't really play so he goes along. To be substitute. Never plays, always picked. Most loyal member of the team. Won player of the season in Year 9. Never played a game.

LEWIS: Good for him. So, he's got a game tonight?

CHLOE: Yeah, only he forgot when he told you to meet him here. In all the excitement of you coming.

LEWIS: Excitement?

CHLOE: You're new and he wants to help you on your way. Because he's a generous guy. And he's something of a control freak.

LEWIS: Great! How d'you know that?

CHLOE: Because I'm his girlfriend.

Pause.

So, he asked me to tell you he's sorry but he can't catch up with you at the end of the day.

LEWIS: Thanks... thanks for telling me.

A pause. Lewis is making to go.

CHLOE: Thanks a lot!

LEWIS: What?

CHLOE: He's stood me up, too.

LEWIS: Oh.

CHLOE: And he always walks me into town, then I catch a bus home.

LEWIS: Sorry.

CHLOE: So, be the gentleman. Walk me into town.

LEWIS: What?

CHLOE: Walk me into town. I'm not gonna walk on my own.

Scene 3 A café in town

It is half an hour later.

LEWIS and CHLOE are just carrying cokes over to a table.

CHLOE: We'll sit here. I like sitting in the window. If your conversation's a bit lacking, I can always watch the world go by.

LEWIS: No pressure on me then.

CHLOE: I'm kidding. So, new boy, how was your day?

LEWIS: Fine. OK really. Nobody stuck my head down the bog!

CHLOE: And Grant was helpful?

LEWIS: Very.

CHLOE: Plenty of advice, I expect.

LEWIS: Yeah, he likes to talk.

CHLOE: What'd he say?

LEWIS: Stuff. Like don't stare at people. Oh - and 'blend'.

CHLOE: Blend?

LEWIS: You know blend, fit in, don't stand out like the 'new kid' or you'll get a beating.

CHLOE: What?

LEWIS: And don't catch people's eye 'cause they're like dogs, or something... they'll attack you.

CHLOE: Dogs? Great! I thought as much.

LEWIS: What?

CHLOE: Doesn't matter. Anyway, where'd you come from?

LEWIS: Hendon.

CHLOE: Where?

LEWIS: North of London.

CHLOE: Oh right. Bit north or lots north?

LEWIS: Bit north. London, really.

CHLOE: And you like our school better, right?

LEWIS: No. Because I've left mates behind there. I've got no friends here.

CHLOE: So, I'm not your friend?

LEWIS: You might be.

CHLOE: Promises!

LEWIS: Another thing - my options. I did French at my last school and French is full here. I have to do Spanish.

CHLOE: And you can't speak any Spanish?

LEWIS: No. My mum's gonna be mad.

CHLOE: Who have you got?

LEWIS: Wait a sec.

He gets out his timetable and, with difficulty, reads the name.

LEWIS: Senora Ortega.

CHLOE: She's all right. Tell her about it. When do you have Spanish?

LEWIS: (*again, checking the timetable*) Tomorrow, first thing.

CHLOE: Grant does Spanish; he can help you. Though he doesn't know as much as he thinks he does.

LEWIS: No?

CHLOE: All this stuff about blending in. It's crap. Being invisible is just being afraid.

LEWIS: Afraid? I thought I blended in so I didn't look afraid.

CHLOE: Look, forget what Grant said. You're the new boy. This is your time.

LEWIS: My time?

CHLOE: It's your moment - so grasp it. You'll not be new for long.

Take us girls. We've known the boys in our year all our lives - there's no mystery, nothing to fancy.

LEWIS: But you're going out with Grant.

CHLOE: That's different. You're the new boy. We don't know you. We can fantasise about you because you could be anything, anything we like. So we're intrigued. And, today, I've done the best thing I can for you.

LEWIS: What?

CHLOE: Sat you here. In the window. You're in the shop window. Every kid at school, every girl, has checked you out as they've gone past.

LEWIS: (*looking out the window*) Yeah?

CHLOE: And they're thinking, 'he's quite something, coming onto Chloe on his first day'.

LEWIS: I'm not. I wouldn't.

CHLOE: You don't fancy me? No, and you know why? Because I'm in control of this little situation. You're just the new boy, right?

LEWIS: This is doing my head in.

CHLOE: Listen. All I'm saying is take your opportunity, make the most of being new. Be noticed, enjoy yourself.

She starts to get up.

CHLOE: And now I'm going.

LEWIS: D'you want me to walk you home?

CHLOE: As if! I can walk home on my own.

LEWIS: But you said...

CHLOE: Oh, Grant... he doesn't really walk me into town. You don't want to believe everything a girl says. You can pay for the cokes though.

She leaves.

Scene 4 The classroom

It is lunchtime the following day, Friday. GRANT is at the teacher's desk once again. He is talking to CHLOE and her friend, ANNA.

CHLOE: You're coming with me Saturday and that's final.

GRANT: I don't feel like it. (*sighs with resignation*) OK.

CHLOE: Now, Anna is interested in your friend, Lewis. So she wants to come with us when we take him out tonight.

ANNA: Just to see what he's like.

LEWIS enters.

GRANT: Lewis, how's things?

LEWIS: OK. Except break.

CHLOE: What?

LEWIS: In the corridor. I got cornered.

GRANT: I knew it! You were staring, weren't you? Looking at them?

LEWIS: I suppose I must have been.

GRANT: They shook you up a bit?

LEWIS: A bit, I guess.

GRANT: What happened?

LEWIS: They came towards me, surrounded me.

GRANT: Where?

LEWIS: History corridor. By the window.

GRANT: Then what?

LEWIS: Then the leader… came up close to me… I could smell…

GRANT: Smell his breath? Disgusting.

LEWIS: No, you don't understand…

GRANT: What did they do?

LEWIS: I'm trying to tell you. Inches from my face. I could smell her breath.

GRANT: Gross!

LEWIS: Then she said...

GRANT: Whoooaa! Rewind.

LEWIS: What?

GRANT: Her breath?

LEWIS: Yes, her breath. That's what I was trying to tell you.

It was this group of girls. They were laughing. They asked me which one I fancied. I said I didn't know. They said I had till lunch to make up my mind, or else! And they laughed and then they walked off.

CHLOE: That leader, did she have blonde hair, big earrings?

LEWIS: Yeah.

CHLOE: Thought so. Charlene Thomas. Just keep them guessing. You can flirt a bit, can't you? By the way, how was Spanish?

LEWIS: OK. That Senora Ortega, she's weird. She told me not to worry. Apparently, it doesn't matter I don't know a single word of Spanish. I'll be fine, she says. I'll be her conquistador.

ANNA: What's that?

LEWIS: Search me. I told you, I don't know a single word of Spanish.

CHLOE: Grant, what's a conquistador?

GRANT: I dunno. I only do ordering drinks in a café, my hobbies and my family.

LEWIS: Right.

GRANT: Anyway, Lewis, be careful round the place, right? You're doing great but if you excite the wrong type of attention, it could all change. Stick to my advice and you'll be fine.

CHLOE frowns at him.

GRANT: By the way, here's a map.

He hands LEWIS a piece of paper.

LEWIS: What? Read it, memorise it, then destroy it?

GRANT: It's a map. How to get to my place. You're coming round. Tonight, about six.

CHLOE: And don't be late. You boys are meeting me and Anna at the bus stop at seven. This, by the way, is Anna.

LEWIS: Hi.

Scene 5 The shed

It is shortly after six that night. GRANT and LEWIS are in the small wooden shed at the back of GRANT's terraced house.

In the middle of the floor is an old motorbike, covered by cloth. Various other shed contents, including tins of parts dismantled from the bike. There are two stools to sit on.

LEWIS: So, now I know one word in Spanish: Conquistador!

GRANT: And it means?

LEWIS: Spanish soldiers who conquered the New World. When America was discovered they went inland. There were only a few dozen of them and they swept across North and South America and they conquered everything they came across - gold and everything. Every race and civilisation.

GRANT: So that's you then? A conqueror. Conquering the new world - this place.

LEWIS: She didn't say that... not really.

GRANT: Just marching in here and conquering everything you come across. Well done! Easy!

LEWIS: What?

GRANT: Nothing.

LEWIS: No, tell me.

GRANT: What I'm saying is: was there a complete idiot getting hold of the Conquistadors and telling them to be invisible? You know: "Don't look anyone in the eye in case they notice you." I'm sure it was practically the Conquistador motto.

LEWIS: She was just trying to convince some poor sod, who didn't know 'Señora' meant 'Mrs', and who has a GCSE in a year and a half, that he can learn Spanish. She knows he hasn't a hope in hell but she doesn't want to hear nothing but whingeing for eighteen months.

GRANT doesn't reply. He has got a tin down off the shelf and is busying himself with its contents.

Grant... she meant conquer Spanish!

GRANT: (*sighs*) She might as well have meant conquer the school. It hasn't exactly been hard, has it? The worst moment so far seems to have been when you were mobbed by half the girls in the year because they all fancy you!

LEWIS: Well, it hasn't happened to me before.

GRANT: Oh, so we're not that choosy either! It's a good job they don't send one of the good looking boys down from Hendon: we'd all fancy him.

LEWIS: (*changing subject*) What's in the tin?

GRANT: Fags. Want one?

LEWIS: Low tar?

GRANT: Roll ups.

LEWIS: Oh.

GRANT: Want one?

LEWIS: Don't smoke.

GRANT: Then why did you...? Doesn't matter.

I like the work that goes into roll ups. I like to make real skinny ones and keep 'em alight because of how well I roll 'em and smoke 'em. Cheap, too.

LEWIS: Can you do smoke rings?

GRANT: No.

LEWIS: Cause it's meant to be easier with rolling tobacco.

GRANT: Yep.

LEWIS: Probably something to do with the thicker smoke. 'Cause it is thicker the way it hangs in the air.

GRANT: Yes, well, I wouldn't know because, as I pointed out, I can't actually blow smoke rings.

Pause.

GRANT: I'm going to give up in a few years. For my health. I reckon I can tell when it's really getting on my lungs when I've smoked a lot. When that's a sort of semi-permanent state I'm giving up - mind over matter. By then, I'll be drinking heavily anyway.

I do a lot of my smoking out here. A roll up is more of a smoke to think by than your average fag, which is more social. Not many people accept a roll up. So I tend to smoke most of them out here.

LEWIS: Does Chloe sit out here with you?

GRANT: Once.

LEWIS: Does your family actually use the shed for anything? Like gardening?

GRANT: No.

LEWIS: (*indicating the cloth-covered object that dominates the shed*) What's this?

GRANT: Matchless G12, 650 twin.

LEWIS: That's a motorbike then?

GRANT: Yeah.

LEWIS: An old one?

GRANT: 1960s.

LEWIS: Does it go?

GRANT: No. It's my dad's. It doesn't go because the last thing he did before he left was strip it down to restore it.

LEWIS: As in left for good?

GRANT: Absolutely for good. Haven't seen him in five years. Not that I blame him. It was hell for him when he tried to keep in touch. So he gave up trying.

LEWIS: Why doesn't your mum get rid of it?

GRANT: Like this it's rusty old junk. Restored, I expect it's worth a small fortune. My step-dad isn't interested. So it stays here. Piece of my dad, still with a foothold in the shed, never to be restored, and managing to be a bloody nuisance to my mum without any effort on his part at all - much like old times.

LEWIS: Why don't you restore it - like a project? Since you're out here a lot anyway and there isn't exactly much else to do.

GRANT: Nah. I'd make a complete mess of it.

Scene 6 The bus shelter

It is about 7.15 that night. GRANT and LEWIS are sitting on the bench in a town bus shelter. It should be somehow clear that they have been sitting here for twenty minutes, and in silence for ten of those minutes.

When CHLOE and ANNA appear, they both sit stiffly up and shift, without speaking, to either end of the bench. CHLOE and ANNA sit in the middle. And give the boys a look.

GRANT: (*by way of explanation for their silence*) Why do you always say "make sure you're on time" and then turn up fifteen minutes late yourself?

CHLOE: You know perfectly well why, Grant. You wouldn't want me sitting here on my own in the town centre, would you?

GRANT: (*reluctantly pursuing a point he knows he can't win*) You had Anna with you...

CHLOE: (*with a quiet note of warning*) Grant!

ANNA: Well, I found out what 'Conquistador' means.

GRANT: Yeah - Spanish conqueror.

ANNA: That's right. It's one of the most shameful episodes in European history, my mum says. Out of monstrous greed, they ransacked a whole continent, killing and raping and destroying some of the most interesting and advanced civilisations in all of human history. They practically wiped out whole native Indian populations with their viruses.

GRANT: I knew it.

ANNA: What?

GRANT: (*indicating LEWIS*) There was something not so flaming perfect about Sir Galahad.

LEWIS: Sir Galahad?!

GRANT: Yeah - stay down your own end of the bench. I don't want a dose of the flu off you. You want to watch yourself, Anna. You might catch something off that conquistador.

LEWIS: Sir Galahad?!

Pause. In the distance, there's a crash, something like a metal bin being thrown over and some shouts. They all look out in the same direction for a moment.

CHLOE: Sid 'n' Nancy.

LEWIS: Who are they?

CHLOE: Him. Sid 'n' Nancy's a bloke. He fancies he runs the town centre in the evenings.

LEWIS: What makes him think that?

CHLOE: Largely, because he does.

GRANT: I just hope he's not coming up this way.

LEWIS: Why's he called Sid 'n' Nancy?

GRANT: No idea. I just hope he doesn't turn up, because I hate having to talk to him. Like he's a mate.

CHLOE: We need to get some drink for this evening, anyway.

LEWIS: Where do you buy drink round here?

GRANT: There's Skanky Pete.

LEWIS: OK. Where's he at?

GRANT: Kebab shop. Roundabout where that bin just took a tumble.

LEWIS: Oh, right.

CHLOE: Come on, Grant. No one really buys drink from Skanky Pete any more. Maybe once when they were twelve. And even then he charged a fiver for the service - which was probably just a bottle of cider.

LEWIS: So, how'd he get the stuff?

CHLOE: He's in the kebab shop, right? You give him a fiver, he goes into the 'offie', buys your cider, goes straight back in the kebab shop, gives you your bottle... and orders himself a large kebab.

You know those big pink meat cakes on a spit in the window. No one ever buys a kebab from those things. Except Skanky Pete. And, I swear, by the end of the evening that thing is skinny as a girl's arm and half the twelve year olds in the town are off their heads.

ANNA: What Chloe is trying to say is that nowadays we don't actually buy our drink from Skanky Pete. We go to the supermarket, we select our choice of alcoholic beverage and we pay for it at the check-out.

CHLOE: Where a row of twenty of our older brothers and sisters sit and process the purchase.

A chorus of shouts is closer.

GRANT: (*looking up the road*) Look, Chloe, we'll go and get something to drink and let these two get to know each other a bit and we'll be right back with something to drink in just a sec.

GRANT stands and CHLOE joins him. They leave. ANNA and LEWIS are alone on the bench.

Another volley of shouts is closer still.

ANNA: We can, if you like, help them carry the bottles.

LEWIS: No. We're all right.

ANNA slides up the bench and takes his arm.
More shouting.

ANNA: Sid 'n' Nancy's coming over.

LEWIS: We're all right.

SID 'N' NANCY comes over on his own. The rest of his group has carried on walking. He likes to keep an eye on his territory. He stands in front of ANNA and LEWIS. They stand up.

ANNA: Sid.

SID: All right, darlin'? And who have we here?

ANNA: This is Lewis. He's new, in our year. He arrived this week.

SID 'N' NANCY reaches out and briefly clasps LEWIS' hand.

SID: All right, man.

Lewis nods.

SID: You the guy comin' onto Chloe first day you're here and now you're with Anna? Cool.

LEWIS: Just getting to know people.

SID: Listen, man, you need anything, you see me. You have any trouble, you speak to me.

LEWIS: Thanks... Sid.

SID: You remember one friggin' thing. You don't ever call me Sid 'n' Nancy, you got that? And you don't ever be smart round me.

LEWIS: Sure.

There are shouts from further down the street.

SID 'N' NANCY looks at them both for a moment and then walks slowly on.

LEWIS and ANNA sit.

Pause.

ANNA: OK?

LEWIS: Fine. I feel great. Listen, did Grant deliberately go off to the supermarket?

ANNA: Yes. He's a very organised guy. He knows just how he likes his life and he steers his way through it. And he's a good friend.

LEWIS: Sure. And, he and Chloe, they've been going out for quite a while?

ANNA: For years. They're very good for each other.

ANNA: Of course, Chloe flirts. And sometimes people get the wrong idea.

LEWIS: Sure.

ANNA: You know that Spanish? I could maybe help you a bit.

LEWIS: You do Spanish?

ANNA: Será mi placer enseñarle español!

LEWIS: Spanish?

ANNA: Si.

LEWIS: What's it mean?

ANNA: It's very advanced, I'm afraid.

LEWIS: You don't know what it means either!

ANNA: You need at least five lessons, and then I'll tell you.

LEWIS stands up, steps back and looks at her for a moment. Then he turns away and flings his arms out wide.

LEWIS: (*shouts*) I am going to conquer the whole new world!

ANNA: Lewis, sit down. What are you playing at?

LEWIS: (*speaks in mock Spanish accent*) I am conquistador. I am going to conquer the new world!

ANNA: Well, I'm not sure I approve. It was one of the most shameful episodes in European history.

LEWIS: (*shouts*) I am going to conquer the new world, but in a nice way. I am conquistador only where all parties are in full agreement!

GRANT and CHLOE are hurrying up to the bus shelter.

GRANT: Lewis, you idiot! I tell you to keep a low profile for a few weeks and, within 24 hours, you're issuing a challenge to all-comers on your first Friday night in the town centre.

Just thank your lucky stars that they've no idea what 'conquistador' means.

(*to Chloe*) This is your fault. Telling him to make his mark.

CHLOE: He's done OK.

LEWIS: Sorry, Grant. I really appreciate all you've...

GRANT: Save the gratitude.

LEWIS: Are you going to drink that here?

GRANT: In the bus shelter?

LEWIS: Well...

GRANT: We're catching the bus up to Sally and George's. They've got a band practice in their dad's garage.

How sad do you think we are?

CHLOE: Last piece of advice, Lewis. Don't answer that question.

THE BOY AT THE HOTEL RUDOLPHO

Characters:

LISA	girl, aged 15
STEFAN	boy, aged 16
KELLY	young receptionist
PAUL	chef in his thirties

The Rudolpho is a medium-to-large seaside hotel that has seen better days. Although half full of guests most of the year, it is struggling to survive. The play is set during a spring/autumn semi-'off season'. We do not venture outside the claustrophobic world of the hotel interior during the course of the play.

Scene 1 A hotel reception

It is early morning, shortly after breakfast has been served. KELLY, the hotel receptionist, is busying herself at the desk when LISA enters.

LISA: Excuse me.

KELLY: Yes?

LISA: My key.

LISA hands her room key to KELLY.

We're going out for the day. I was wondering... if you had any information... about places to visit.

KELLY: There's a selection of leaflets in the lounge.

STEFAN enters the reception area from the back office.

STEFAN: I'll take over here, Kelly.

Surprisingly, Kelly shows no reaction to this instruction from someone clearly younger. She exits into the back office.

STEFAN: Now, how exactly can we help?

LISA: (*taken aback for a moment*) Well, we're here for a few days. And we want to check out some places to visit.

STEFAN: That's you and your parents?

LISA: My parents?

STEFAN: Saw you going into breakfast.

LISA: Right.

STEFAN: And you're going to the castle today?

LISA: Maybe.

STEFAN: Everybody does. I'll get together some places to visit - what to see when it's raining, when it's fine, stuff with culture, places with views - everything your parents will enjoy.

LISA: And me?

STEFAN: You'll enjoy some. But today - the castle. Don't go.

LISA: What?

STEFAN: Don't go. Look...

He seeks out and presents Lisa with a leaflet about the castle.

STEFAN: It's nice, isn't it? The walls, the towers, the slitty windows...

LISA: Yes.

STEFAN: Well, that's it. That's all there is. But your parents will walk slowly round every bit of it, trying to absorb... history.

LISA: How do you know?

STEFAN: That's what people their age do. As for you, look at the picture. There's a nice sunset. But you won't get that today. You've seen it at its best. So don't go.

LISA: I might be interested in history.

STEFAN: You might be. So don't go.

LISA: That doesn't make sense.

STEFAN: Look, nothing ever happened there. It's just a posh house someone built. Then, gradually, it fell down. Now, it's just walls. You can't go there and see what it used to be like. But some people feel obliged to try... 'how people used to live'.

STEFAN: Anyway, your parents will want to spend some time on their own.

LISA: Oh, yeah!

STEFAN: Second honeymoon.

LISA is surprised.

They told Kelly before breakfast. So, tricky call for you to make - the ultimate gooseberry, a child at your parents' honeymoon.

LISA: Oi!

Pause.

It's just a holiday really.

STEFAN: Listen. Let your parents go to the castle. Stay here. Tell them you want to finish your book.

LISA: Maybe I don't read.

STEFAN: But you do.

LISA: Yeah?

STEFAN: Girls like you always read.

STEFAN: Listen, don't go to the castle. Stay here. Read the book. And, at 11, come down and have coffee with me in the lounge.

LISA: And that's supposed to be more exciting?

STEFAN: I'll promise you... some real history.

LISA: (*looks for a moment, puzzling him out*) In the lounge?

STEFAN: 11 o'clock. Kelly...

KELLY comes out as STEFAN exits into the back office.

Lisa would like her room key.

KELLY offers LISA the key. After a moment, she takes it.

Scene 2 The lounge

It is 11 o'clock. STEFAN and LISA are seated in comfortable chairs. They are in a corner of the lounge. A murmuring of other guests may be heard at intervals during the scene. At the table before them is a coffee set. STEFAN is pouring coffee for LISA.

STEFAN: (*as he pours cream into his own coffee*) I do enjoy serving coffee from a pot.

LISA: Yes. More of an occasion.

STEFAN: More of a ceremony than a quenching of thirst. Not like crashing water into a glass and chucking it down your neck while still standing at the sink. And still holding onto the tap.

LISA: More about... the people you're with.

Pause.

Listen. I'm having coffee with you. But I don't know your name. It seems kind of wrong somehow!

STEFAN: Stefan.

LISA: You had me at a disadvantage for a while back there. I didn't know your name... but you knew mine.

STEFAN: Hmm?

LISA: You called me 'Lisa'. At Reception.

STEFAN: I did?

LISA: You did.

STEFAN: I must have checked your name in the register. It's a careless habit. Disconcerting?

LISA: A bit.

STEFAN: I'm sorry.

LISA: So, do you work here or what?

STEFAN: I live here.

LISA: In the hotel?

STEFAN: My uncle's the manager. We have a flat upstairs. Which he thinks is one of the great benefits of the job, along with never having to cook a meal.

LISA: What do you think?

STEFAN: It's just an excuse for him to work 24/7.

LISA: And you live with your uncle all the time?

STEFAN: Yes.

LISA: And your parents?

Pause.

STEFAN: Can I tell you about that... when I know you better?

LISA: Sure.

Pause.

STEFAN: So your parents have gone to the castle?

LISA: Yeah.

STEFAN: And you've been reading your book?

LISA: As instructed!

STEFAN: Let me guess what it was... it was... a horror?

LISA: Yeah, kind of. How d'you know that?

STEFAN: By looking at you. Reading you.

LISA: Reading me? Like a book?

STEFAN: Little bit.

LISA: (*amused*) That easy!

STEFAN: Not that easy. Horror is boys' reading.

LISA: Get out of here! It's girls that read horror.

LISA: Always have done. Girls are fascinated by situations of fear. Look, take fairs - they're all about girls, girls screaming.

STEFAN: No, they're not.

LISA: Oh, boys go there to pose. But it's girls who ride. Girls who love the rides.

STEFAN: They just like the lads on the rides chatting them up.

LISA: It's more than that. It's being scared but safe.

STEFAN: We all like that.

LISA: It's different for girls. Like horror stories. I can be entering the graveyard at midnight, and reading a book at midday, in the same moment - scared and safe.

Mind you, it's books that make graveyards frightening. I reckon I wouldn't be scared in a real graveyard at night.

STEFAN: (*unconvinced*) Oh, yeah!

LISA: In real life, I know the dead won't come up out of the ground. But, in a book, there's different rules.

STEFAN: Have you ever been alone at night?

LISA: No, but I have been outside at night. Camping. Have you ever been awake in the early hours?

STEFAN: Yeah.

LISA: Not indoors. But outside. On the ground. Between, say, one and four. Time which doesn't exist... for nearly everyone in the world. And you're on the ground. In touch with the Earth. And, if you concentrate, for... maybe ten minutes... you can begin to feel the Earth turning so fast... so fast it makes you want to grab onto the grass with your fingers... and hold on.

Anyway, this was your idea.

You promised me real history?

STEFAN: Hmm?

LISA: If I didn't go to the castle – real history.

STEFAN: Right. Well, real history is going on all the time. It's us. Not walls. Not trying to guess what people used to do inside walls. But what they're doing now, here in the lounge, in the corridor, behind closed doors.

LISA: But that's not history - that's now.

STEFAN: The moment you do something it's in the past and it has consequences for the future.

LISA: So?

STEFAN: So, sit here and look. At the people. There's nowhere like a hotel for looking at people. Granted, they think they're on best behaviour so no one can guess what's going on with them. But you watch them and you can.

LISA: And that's what you do? When you're working here?

STEFAN: I don't exactly work here. But it's what I do to pass the time.

LISA: You must be really bored.

STEFAN: No, it's interesting. People live the bits of their lives when life's 'on hold' at home. When they come to hotels they stop and they can't help taking stock. Things happen.

LISA: (*looking around*) Well, it doesn't look like that to me. There's nothing happening.

STEFAN: It looks like nothing. And they all seem to come for the same things. Old people come for food, young couples for sex and kids come for adventure. Well, they're certainly disappointed! Like you could be - if I don't take you in hand!

LISA: I'm not a kid!

STEFAN: People come for those things but something else shifts in their lives while they're here.

Look at those two by the window. They just look bored. And they are. But they're only just realising that. They didn't know that till they came. And now they're alone together, with nothing else but themselves, they're finding out they've got nothing left to keep them together.

LISA: Good guess work.

STEFAN: No. It's not speculation... I know. Like sometimes you come across people and they're in trouble. You know because you're watching them like no one else is. But no one else knows. You want to tell someone because you don't know what to do. But you're only watching, you can't intervene. You can't help people, can you, if you're watching them in secret?

STEFAN: Because strictly speaking you shouldn't know what you do know.

LISA looks at him to see what he means.

STEFAN: Look. Will you meet me at 4.30?

LISA: Why 4.30?

Pause.

STEFAN: I want to tell you about... my parents.

LISA: OK.

STEFAN: Go up to your floor. Walk to the back stairs, up to the next floor, along that corridor to the end by the lift, and go back down to your floor. And go round again. I'll find you.

LISA: Why the mystery?

STEFAN: I'm going to show you a place in the hotel. I don't want anyone else to know.

Pause.

LISA: OK.

STEFAN gets up to leave.

STEFAN: Thanks. I enjoyed having coffee with you.

LISA: Me too.

STEFAN: See you at 4.30. Don't be late.

Scene 3 The laundry room

It is 4.30. STEFAN is in the laundry room. He is shaking out sheets, scrunching them into balls and piling them into a corner. He is making what is effectively a nest of freshly laundered sheets.

(In staging terms, the armchairs from the previous scene can have a couple of duvets laid over them and STEFAN can throw a couple of sheets on top.)

Once satisfied with the result, he goes to the door and, as LISA passes (off stage), he pulls her into the room. She is shocked both by the suddenness of the physical contact and her arrival in, what appears to be, a cupboard.

LISA: Hey!

STEFAN: Sorry.

LISA: This is silly! You're being silly, Stefan.

STEFAN: I just don't want anyone to know I come here.

LISA: Into a cupboard?

STEFAN: It's the laundry room.

LISA: You shouldn't have grabbed me like that. What's so special about a laundry room?

STEFAN: It's a busy place all day. But, after four, no one comes here. Except me. And no one knows I come here.

LISA: Look, I'm sorry. Thank you for bringing me to... the laundry room!

STEFAN: Sit here.

STEFAN sits himself down in the nest of sheets and turns to LISA, who remains where she stands.

LISA: No thanks. I'm not sure if I want to be in a cupboard with someone I hardly know, let alone get into some bed sheets with him. If no one knows you're here, they don't know I am either. Besides, they'll be disgusting: anyone could have slept in those!

STEFAN: No one has. They're all fresh.

LISA: You'll get into trouble with the housekeeper.

STEFAN: Nah! I just put them in the dirty laundry baskets - no one counts; no one's any the wiser.

LISA: How often do you do this?

STEFAN: Just sometimes. When I feel low.

LISA: Why?

STEFAN: Because... they smell good and I sink into them and they give me comfort. And I'm a sicko loser and a freak!

And... there isn't anyone who actually hugs me... so I have to... kind of hug myself.

LISA walks over and sits down in the nest of sheets, but not actually touching STEFAN.

LISA: It does smell good. It's soft and smells of steam and linen and those best nights of getting into bed. And mothers.

She looks at him suddenly.

It smells of mothers, doesn't it?

STEFAN: (*in a weaker voice*) It does.

Pause.

LISA: What happened to your parents, Stefan?

Long pause.

STEFAN: I never knew my father. I don't know what happened to him. I don't know for sure he's dead. But he is dead.

He died just outside Srebrenica. Heard of it?

LISA: No.

STEFAN: Srebrenica is in Bosnia. When I was young, a civil war erupted and, in the summer of 1995, my family were refugees in Srebrenica under the protection of Dutch UN troops. My family are Muslims. The Serbs attacked; the UN gave way; women and children were deported; and, about 7,000 men - mostly fathers - were massacred.

My mother and I came to Britain to make a new life.

She wasn't strong. She didn't survive.

LISA: I'm so sorry, Stefan. I don't know what to say.

And you came to live with your uncle here in the hotel?

STEFAN: Yes.

LISA: And he survived the massacre?

STEFAN: Yes. No. He didn't. He wasn't there. His was a different story. A different story.

LISA: It's OK.

She reaches forward and kisses him on the forehead.

STEFAN: You see, when you talk about loving horror and being scared and safe at the same time, I know what you mean. But I know there's also scared and not safe. And I feel guilty about being scared... and safe. It doesn't feel right... to be safe.

I couldn't walk through a graveyard because the dead would rise up in my own head. And the history of old walls doesn't interest me. The history that matters is the history of people still walking around. Or people who should still be walking around. The history of us.

LISA: I'm sorry.

STEFAN: Don't you feel sorry. What have you done? There's no point in guilt and I shouldn't be laying all this stuff on you.

So - I'm going to make it up to you. I'm going to take you to dinner. Tonight.

LISA: I'm sorry, Stefan. I can't *not* go to dinner with my parents. Not going to the castle is one thing but not going to dinner as well...

Maybe I can see you tomorrow.

STEFAN: No. It has to be tonight.

LISA: I can't.

STEFAN: It has to be tonight. Look. Go to dinner with your parents but don't eat.

LISA: I can't do that.

STEFAN: I mean: don't eat much. Order fish. Order salad. Order fruit.

LISA: And?

STEFAN: At midnight, come back down. Back to the dining room.

LISA: What for?

STEFAN: Dinner.

LISA: At midnight?

STEFAN: Yes.

LISA: Dinner?

STEFAN: Leave it to me.

LISA: I can't. It's crazy. I've got to go.

LISA gets up to go.

My parents will be back.

STEFAN: You've got to come.

LISA: (*at the door*) I'm sorry, Stefan.

STEFAN: I'm going to be organising it all evening.

He gets up.

I'm doing it for you.

LISA has gone.

Scene 4 The dining room

It is midnight in the hotel dining room. The rest of the room is in darkness. STEFAN sits at the one table for two lit by candles. It is perfectly laid and a simple starter is placed either side of the table.

STEFAN is sitting, slumped. He has been here some time but is doggedly waiting. He is wearing a tuxedo.

With the silence and the darkness, a deep stillness has settled on the scene.

Long pause.

From within the upstage darkness, LISA makes her way tentatively forward. STEFAN does not see or hear her.

She, too, has made an effort to dress for dinner.

LISA: Stefan?

She waits just short of the table.

STEFAN: (*standing*) You came.

LISA: I couldn't stand you up. Not at midnight.

STEFAN walks round and pulls back a chair for her. She sits. He returns to his seat and stands for a moment behind it.

STEFAN: Thanks.

Pause.

STEFAN: I promised you adventure.

LISA: You did. And food, too!

She realises the other option was sex. An awkward pause.

I didn't mean... You know...

STEFAN: No. Nor me.

Pause.

STEFAN: This is my best day though.

LISA: I didn't expect anything like this. Is there really... dinner?

STEFAN: Yes. Just a moment.

STEFAN leaves. LISA waits. After a moment, he returns and sits.

LISA: What was that?

STEFAN: The chef.

LISA: There's a chef?

STEFAN: Yes. He's cooking two steaks. You eat steak, I hope?

LISA: A small one.

STEFAN: Wine?

LISA: Thanks.

He pours a glass for each of them.

LISA: Here we are, playing at grown-ups again.

STEFAN: Cheers.

They drink.

STEFAN: Let's eat.

They begin the starters.

LISA: What kind of chef is it that cooks for some boy at midnight, even if he is the manager's nephew?

STEFAN: I know some things. Deals that Paul does with the butcher. It's all very harmless but he'd rather people didn't know.

LISA: People like your uncle, for instance?

STEFAN: Maybe.

LISA: You're not close to your uncle, are you?

STEFAN: No.

Pause.

LISA: Are you sure we won't be found out?

STEFAN: The bar's at the other end of the hotel. No one comes down here at night.

Pause.

How are you finding midnight in a hotel dining room?

LISA: What?

STEFAN: Compared to, say, a graveyard?

LISA: Oh God! Nothing like. Though it is dark and I feel I should be very quiet.

STEFAN: Scared and safe?

LISA: Scared and not quite safe from being caught.

STEFAN: Better than scared and safe?

LISA: I don't know. Oh, boys! You have no imagination. The danger's got to be real for you. You just can't do 'pretend'.

PAUL enters with two plates of steak. He puts them down and picks up the starter plates.

PAUL: Everything all right?

LISA: Very nice. It's very good of you.

STEFAN: Paul, this is Lisa.

PAUL: Hi. I'm just pleased he's found someone of his own age to talk to. Bit of a loner, our Stefan.

Look, if you're OK, Stef, I'm off.

STEFAN: Fine. Thanks, Paul.

PAUL: Right. Goodnight. Enjoy.

(*As PAUL exits.*)

LISA: Goodnight.

STEFAN: See ya.

They eat.

STEFAN: This thing about not safe. There has to be a bit of an edge otherwise it's just not scary. Not in the way that churns your insides.

LISA: Lovely!

STEFAN: Do you know that feeling that comes with danger, real danger?

LISA: I think I know what you mean, yes.

STEFAN: I have to have that.

LISA: Real danger?

STEFAN: That feeling that comes with danger.

LISA: Fear?

STEFAN: Fear... and excitement, mixed.

LISA: And where does that come from?

Pause.

STEFAN: It's a secret. I haven't told anyone else.

LISA: What?

STEFAN: If I tell you, you mustn't tell anyone else.

LISA: I don't know.

STEFAN: And you'll have to promise to do it with me.

LISA: What?

STEFAN: Do it with me.

LISA: Do what?

STEFAN: I can't tell you.

LISA: Well, I can't 'do it with you'! I don't like the sound of it anyway.

Pause.

LISA: (*sighs*) All right. I promise not to tell anyone.

STEFAN: Really promise?

LISA: Really promise.

But I can't do it, whatever it is. I can't promise that.

STEFAN: OK. You know I told you I watch people - try to work them out?

LISA: Yes.

STEFAN: That people are at a moment in their lives. Of change or something.

LISA: Yes.

STEFAN: Well, that's rubbish. You can't tell that from watching people walk through the lobby or order breakfast.

LISA: No?

STEFAN: Oh, you can detect an atmosphere sometimes or see they're in love or you can see the type of people they are - timid or snobs or all for show...

LISA: Isn't that it though? Isn't that reading people, working them out? Snob, unhappy, in love?

STEFAN: But it's not enough.

LISA: What do you mean?

STEFAN: I mean that I see so many people and they all seem to fit into types. But people aren't types, are they? There's something unique about everyone, isn't there?

LISA: Is there? Who knows?

STEFAN: I think I do.

LISA: What?

STEFAN: I think I know.

LISA: How?

STEFAN: By looking further. You have to see more than the public face.

LISA: People give themselves away?

STEFAN: In private they do.

LISA: Oh my God! You don't spy on people, do you? Through the keyhole?

STEFAN: No.

LISA: You're not a pervert?

STEFAN: No. I perform a service at the hotel.

LISA: What?!

STEFAN: Please listen. I think it's called 'adding value'. I do something to make this place just a little bit classier. Like the best hotels.

LISA: What?

STEFAN: I fold down the sheets.

LISA: Is that it?

STEFAN: Like in good hotels. You come up after dinner and someone has been in, folded down the corner of the top sheet, maybe turned on a table lamp. Made it feel special. It's like good linen and deep carpets and heavy curtains.

LISA is still not convinced.

It's those touches that make a hotel worth paying for.

Some places make the mistake of trying to offer a home from home. They interfere when people want to be anonymous. They make it cluttered and chintzy when all you want to do is get away from clutter. You can't get away from it at home because clutter at home is your life. You just want a break from it.

And in hotels you want to be treated like you're somebody... like a lord.

STEFAN: In the old country house, someone would come into her ladyship's bedroom and stoke up the fire and tidy the dresser and turn down the bed.

LISA: OK. You turn down the bed.

STEFAN: And...

LISA: There's more?

STEFAN: While I'm there, I might notice things.

LISA: Notice?

STEFAN: Look around.

LISA: Oh God. I was right. You *are* a pervert. Sniffing round! Sniffing round their bed linen!

She stands up.

STEFAN: (*his voice raised*) Sit down! (*more quietly*) Sit down!

LISA freezes.

The least you can do is hear me out. I've opened up my whole life to you. And all you do is make some nasty judgement on me.

STEFAN: You owe me a fair hearing. Please, sit down. Just for two minutes.

She sits. Reluctantly.

Of course, I wouldn't snoop on anyone. I wouldn't go into their homes, but they're in a hotel. Their room is private and public in a way, too. Well, it's public to the servant class.

The maid, the cleaner, the handy man, any of them would be expected to go in. And they're bound to know some things about people in a hotel. Everyone accepts that.

In the old country house, do you think the servants didn't know every little detail of the family's business? Of course they did. The family were like actors or celebrities in their own home. They lived with their notoriety amongst the servants. Lived with it.

I just happen to know some things that servants know and when people leave the hotel they're none the wiser. No harm done.

LISA: OK. Look, I'm just tired. It's been a long day.

She gets up to leave.

STEFAN: Lisa, let me prove it to you. Turn down the beds with me tomorrow. Tomorrow at eight.

LISA: I don't know. Goodnight, Stefan.

LISA turns to walk back through the dining room. She seems suddenly very tired.

STEFAN: The thing is. The thing I didn't say… I need your help.

She stops.

I need someone like you, someone who's not me, to come, to help me decide what to do. I need all your doubt, all your scruples. I need you to come precisely because you don't want to come. Please.

She half turns.

I asked you once what you do if you find out someone you're watching is in trouble. And you're not supposed to know.

I think someone in the hotel is in trouble. I think I'm the only person who knows it. And I don't know what I'm supposed to do.

LISA: All right. I'll come.

She walks away, out of the dining room.

STEFAN sits and reaches for the bottle again.

Scene 5 A guest bedroom

The room is almost dark. Upstage centre is a bed. Downstage centre, a small bureau.

STEFAN and LISA enter. STEFAN goes straight to the bureau and switches on the lamp. LISA is at his side.

LISA: This is the last one. They'll be coming up from dinner any minute.

STEFAN: And?

LISA: And they'll catch us.

STEFAN: And we'll say: "Good evening. Just doing the lamps and the bed. Is there anything else you require this evening?"

LISA: I'm so nervous my stomach is churning. I want to go to the toilet.

STEFAN: There's one just there, en suite.

LISA: You're crazy.

STEFAN: Listen. I told you, this guy is in trouble.

LISA looks over his shoulder.

Some things in these papers he's left out. He doesn't go anywhere but he has these out every night. Things underlined. Just let me find the page...

LISA: Honestly, Stefan, we can't look through his papers.

STEFAN: Well, turn down the bed then.

LISA turns to go back up to the bed.

He keeps coming back to...

A muffled gasp from LISA makes STEFAN turn and, as she speaks, move to the other side of the bed.

LISA: (*in a hoarse whisper*) This one's not empty. He's asleep.

They are transfixed by the figure in the bed.

(*beginning to move very slowly towards the door*) Come on, Stef.

STEFAN: Lisa, don't.

He moves towards the figure in the bed.

He's not asleep.

He bends down, takes hold of the wrist lying on top of the covers.

He's not asleep. He's dead.

Scene 6 The lounge

It is late the following morning. STEFAN is seated. LISA comes over to join him. She is dressed for going out.

LISA: I've come to say goodbye.

He does not acknowledge her.

My parents want to take me home now.

What we did was wrong. Maybe maids go into people's rooms. We shouldn't have intruded on that scene.

STEFAN: Grave suddenly open up in the night and scare you, Lisa? People don't just die in books; they can die right there in front of you.

LISA: I spoke to your father this morning.

STEFAN: What? Oh, my step-father you mean.

LISA: You lied to me.

STEFAN: So, my real father didn't die in Srebrenica?

LISA: He did. But your mother remarried... a British soldier... who became a hotel manager.

Your mother didn't die, did she, Stef? She left, both of you. Two years ago. One minute she was wife, mother and housekeeper and the next, gone.

STEFAN: How clever of you.

LISA: Don't say that.

STEFAN: Feel better for knowing? For prying into my secrets?

LISA: Look, my parents are in the car.

STEFAN: You'd better go then.

LISA: I feel for what you've been through. But you've got to get out, start living your own life, and not other people's.

STEFAN: Don't you dare be so smug! Look at your own life first, Lisa. Look at your family life and your books!

LISA: That's not fair!

I didn't want to say this. But maybe you should hear what it feels like to have someone inspect your life.

Last night, when I got to bed, something struck me for the first time. You see, you were so right. Something I liked about staying here... every evening, when I got into my room, I found someone had thoughtfully turned down the corner of the sheets.

You.

And now I want to burn every book, every stitch of clothing, every single thing you ran your grubby little fingers through.

STEFAN: I promise I never touched any of your stuff.

LISA: I don't believe you. You said it: you are a sicko freak. And I hope this stops you before you do something really twisted.

Enter KELLY.

KELLY: (*to LISA*) Your parents were wondering...

LISA: I'm just coming.

Exit KELLY.

LISA waits for a moment for STEFAN to speak.

LISA: Nothing to say all of a sudden?

STEPHAN: What's the point? You won't believe me, whatever I say.

LISA: Maybe that's the point. I never will.

LISA gets up and leaves.

STEFAN remains seated where she leaves him.